CITY KIDS
in
CHINA

Also by Peggy Thomson

AUKS, ROCKS AND THE ODD DINOSAUR
Inside Stories from the Smithsonian's Museum of Natural History
KEEPERS AND CREATURES AT THE NATIONAL ZOO

CITY KIDS

in

CHINA

PEGGY THOMSON

photographs by

PAUL S. CONKLIN

HarperCollins*Publishers*

Printed in the United States of America. For information address
HarperCollins Children's Books, a division of HarperCollins Publishers,
10 East 53rd Street, New York, NY 10022.
Typography by Christine Kettner
1   2   3   4   5   6   7   8   9   10

Library of Congress Cataloging-in-Publication Data
Thomson, Peggy.
    City kids in China / Peggy Thomson ; photographs by Paul Conklin.
        p.   cm.
    Summary: A description of what life is like in the modern Chinese
city of Changsha for the children who live there.
    ISBN 0-06-021654-9. —ISBN 0-06-021655-7 (lib. bdg.)
    1. Children—China—Ch' ang-sha shih—Juvenile literature.
2. Ch' ang-sha shih (China)—Description—Juvenile literature.
[1. China—Social life and customs.]   I. Conklin, Paul, ill.
II. Title.
HQ792.C5T46   1991   90-1993
305.23'0951—dc20   CIP
                                                                AC

for editor Barbara Fenton,
who listened to our pretrip quaverings and said: Go

for teenager Chen-wen, met in the market,
who said: I will walk with you

for friend Ellen Roberts, who looked at pictures and journals,
and saw stacks of Fun, and 2 Good 2 Lose, and Boring

Contents

NOTE: Paragraphs in *italics* throughout the book were written in English by Chinese children (most of them thirteen-year-olds) in the English classes of Ya-li Middle School in Changsha. Teacher: Alex Wilmerding.

CITY KIDS
in
CHINA

⌐⌐

Introduction

THE CHINESE CITY of Changsha is circled all about with the green
of rice fields, where water buffaloes and farmers in umbrella hats
slog knee-deep through mud. The city itself is gray and it's gritty,
mostly because of coal dust floating in the air from cookstoves and
from factories. People here cough the grit from their throats and
scrub it from clothes in a *mei yu ban fa* ("it can't be helped") manner.

They say they like everything about their city—except the coal
dust, of course, and the weather. The weather here is hot a lot—
either wet hot, in spring, when wash is soggy for a week, or dry
dusty hot, in summer. Wintertime's sleet and raw cold require layers
of clothes, socks on top of socks, and shirts and pants over sweat
suits. Changsha folk say their city is blessed with two fine days in

October—cool, crisp, clear—when the maples turn scarlet. But not every October. They say: Don't count on it.

Changsha has acres of apartments—cement look-alikes—and great numbers of trucks and of buses, bulging with passengers, and out on the streets a million bicyclists *chingching*ing their bicycle bells. People on foot, school kids among them, dart alongside the traffic. At the giant railway station, great crowds wait at the ticket windows. Chinese cities are like this.

But Changsha is also special. It's special for the big smooth river running through it and the sandbar island in the river, which has orange trees and a roller-skating rink. Crossing the bridge—on foot, by bike—is an adventure.

Changsha is special for Yuelu Mountain on the far bank of the river, which has a temple on it and tombs and stone lions and a bamboo puzzle maze to get lost in. Students, escaping crowded dorm rooms, come here to wander the shady paths and read aloud to trees.

Schools are special in Changsha also. The university at the foot of Yuelu celebrated its thousandth birthday—a world record. One high school trains boys and girls to perform operas and to do dazzling shadow-puppet shows and to make all the fierce-looking fast moves of *wushu*, which looks like fighting but is more a dance than a fight.

In this city, people are experts at crafts. Carvers carve the roots of bamboo into rumpled-looking beasts. Stitchers in the big embroidery factory stitch fine pictures of bears, birds, and fish onto the tops of quilts. Fur, feathers, and scales look like the real thing. Dewdrops shine on petals.

A sign of importance—Changsha is capital of its province. The province, called Hunan, is southerly, about on a level with Florida.

CHINA

China has always called itself the Middle Kingdom, or Middle Country, and looked on people from beyond its borders as barbarians or, at best, an odd lot of foreigners.

The first of the two picture-word characters for writing Middle Country is an easy-to-recognize target, pierced by an arrow.

中 国

CHANGSHA

Roughly in the middle of this Middle Country of China is the city of Changsha, which is a night-and-day train ride from the seacoast, from Beijing to the north, from Shanghai to the east.

The city was named for its sandbar island in the river, *chang* meaning "long" and *sha* meaning "sand." Changsha is pronounced like a double sneeze, with the *a*'s as in Ah! Ah! and the accent on both syllables, the *chang* as strong as the *sha*.

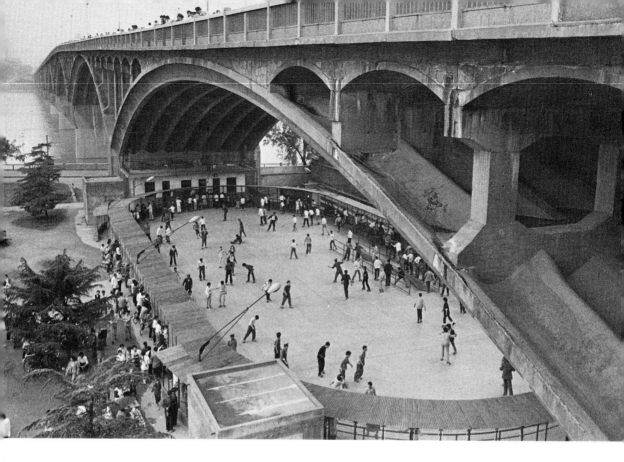

It's as big as the state of Kansas (but with twenty-five times more people) and is a huge producer of food. Like the Kansas wheatlands, which are a "breadbasket" for America, Hunan is a "rice bowl" for China and has as well millions of prize pigs, and ducks and fish, quantities of tea, too, and cotton, bamboo, minerals, and wood.

Here in Changsha, farmers are forever bringing greens into the city, or baskets of cheeping chicks hung from carrying poles across their shoulders. People of Changsha expect to see them and to have farm smells in their nostrils and farm muck underfoot. They count their blessings not to live in the green fields, knee-deep in mud. But they brag about their old home villages and are aware every day of bounty from the countryside.

In city markets people buy live eels and garlics fresh from the country. In factories they fashion local metals into machine parts and bamboo into hats and mats. People see, on the river, barges riding low in the water with cargo of their province. They hear trains in the night, whistling, moving out with long lines of boxcars.

In Changsha the food is hot. Pepper floats in the smoke of kitchens, and cooks sneeze mightily. The eyes of diners prickle even before food reaches the table. The food is peppery and the people are peppery also. They're quick to speak out—open and direct—which is why Changsha may have more than its share of leaders.

The giant among these is Mao Tse-tung. Mao had pepper baked into his bread. He said pepper eaters made good revolutionaries. It was Mao—bluff, brave, shrewd, and ruthless—who led his band of followers across raging rivers and ranges of mountains. It was Mao who led hundreds of millions of Chinese peasants out of deepest poverty to a life where they could expect food, and medical care and schools. From the time of the Communists' victory in 1949 until his death in 1976, he was head of the government under its new red flag and its new name: the People's Republic of China.

People in Changsha tell how Mao walked as a boy to their city from his farm village forty miles away. He saw his first newspapers here. He studied and taught. In roughest weather, Mao and his friends climbed Yuelu Mountain and camped and swam off the tip of Orange Island, toughening up on purpose for the hardships to come. People tell how Mao admired George Washington for his stubbornness and for his skill at guerilla warfare. They show the restaurant that brags "Chairman Mao Ate Here!" and keeps his favorite meal on the menu, though the name for it means "hot foul-smelling bean curd."

7

The memory of Mao is only half proud. For he ruled badly and with an "iron wrist," and many of his programs were disasters. In the mid-1960s he sent out teenage Red Guards, wearing red armbands, to ransack houses and burn books and parade teachers through streets in dunce caps and break up families, sending people to hard labor—on suspicion of disloyalty. The persecuted people had "old" thoughts or "bad" (that is, educated or well off) family. Or they were "stinking thinkers."

Since Mao's death, the photographs of him that hung in every home and office and classroom have vanished. So have most of the statues. People don't forgive or forget the awful times at the end of his life—the cruelties and the suffering that did not have to be. ("Ten years of chaos! Let it never come again!") But people of the city are ever proud the new China got its start with them.

In this city, far in China's interior, Americans are still not an everyday sight. They're rare enough on the street to be looked at and laughingly called the "big noses" (for their craggy features) or the "glass eyes" (for their blue eyes). They are run after by youngsters calling out "Good-a-bye, hallo, hallo, hallo," and pounced on by students who fall into step with them along the sidewalk in order to try out their English conversation or a few bars of "Home on the Range." Here Tom Sawyer, Abe Lincoln, and Martin Luther King are greatly admired; break dancers also. Mickey Mouse and Donald Duck are adored, as they are everywhere by Chinese.

In a daily way, even on trips to school, down market lanes and past factories and along crowded boulevards, the boys and girls who live here come to know their ordinary and their special city.

From a 2000-year-old woman in the museum the children know some glories of their past. They look down at her through her bubble glass dome, at her boniness and her gold brown skin. Everything about her—because she was swaddled in layers of cotton and packed in white clay and charcoal—is perfectly preserved. She's an oddity and a treasure.

Her belongings, all on show, are treasures also. She has her flutes and lacquer bowls and swords and mirrors decorated with dragons, even jaunty little carved musicians, sent along on her journey into the cosmos. She has dried food too (a homey pancake for comfort), and gauzy garments. Her silk banner is painted with the sun and the moon and a hibiscus tree and a portrait of herself, leaning on her cane. China is poor today, but 2000 years ago it had all this in the city of Changsha when North America was still wilderness.

Straight from wrinkled old-timers, children know about the last emperor and how he was toppled in 1911 and the first shots were fired for a people's government. They hear about the city's old stone wall, and the nine clanking gates, and the streets so narrow then that people talked to each other across them from second-story porches. From grandparents and parents children know of warlord wars, and of fires and bombs during World War II, and of the long, bitter civil war, when members of families were often enemies to each other—on opposing sides.

Children live close to their parents, in crowded small rooms, and have heard the tales ten thousand times. They've watched their parents laugh sometimes in the telling of long-ago adventure and seen their eyes blaze with pride or with the thrill or fright of it. Other times they've seen mothers and fathers go quiet with re-membered pain and disappointment.

The city kids in these pages know the heroes to whom they owe their schools and bikes and the calm of their everyday lives. No one blames the young for not having "tasted bitterness" as the grown-ups have had to do. No one urges boys and girls to be

heroes. Young people's work, they understand, is to be wide-awake in school and to stay well and, through all they do, to keep alive the traditions. of music and puppets and fine writing with ink and brush, fine *wushu* moves with their bodies. In a Chinese city, young people are to live in harmony with their families. That's a Chinese tradition also.

FLYING DRAGON OF YELLOW EARTH HILL

A schoolboy, Flying Dragon, writing his name and address on an envelope or inside a notebook, puts his country first and himself last—upside down from the Western way. He puts China on the top line, below it the province, the city, then his neighborhood (which is the walled-off compound called Yellow Earth Hill) and his parents' work unit, and the apartment building. Last, at the bottom, his name—family name first, then given name. (A Chinese woman keeps her own family name when she marries; children take the family name of the father.)

中华人民共和国

湖南省　长沙市　黄土岭

湖南省广播电视厅

三栋一单元

任龙飞

Playing Farmer and Sheep (which is often called Eagle and Chicks), children first mill around, then form into a swishing chain to keep Farmer from tagging them.

C H A P T E R

1

Comrades by the Shirttails

THE SOUND of young voices, singing, leads to a door open to the street. Here in the playrooms of a child-care center, the Ones and Twos are rolling squishy balls or they're sitting on laps, dreaming. The Threes and Fours, in a circle of little chairs, are lustily singing. Chins up, mouths wide, they sing "School Is My Home." They sing rice-planting songs, a hand-washing song, a Chinese-style "Eensy Weensy Spider Went up the Water Spout." To piano tunes they bend and stretch, circle right and left, march two by two.

This center, in the Yellow Earth Hill compound, is for families who live here in the quiet blocks of apartments. The parents work for the radio and TV station on the top of the hill (or one parent works for the station and the other pedals out to a job in another

THE RED KERCHIEF

Ou Si-wei's kerchief shows he is a Young Pioneer. It's red, to represent a corner of the Chinese flag, and it's his to wear always as a mark of honor. He wears the kerchief over his school clothes and also, as he's pictured here, over his costume for a dance at school. His costume is a pint-size army uniform—real People's Liberation Army green, with brass buttons and red trim. Only two weeks before, Ou Si-wei's teacher tied the kerchief on him for the first time, and the boy ran all the way home to show his mother. Few children win the kerchief so young. "How was I picked? Well, how is anyone? I'm seven. You have to be seven [up to fourteen] and get good scores and be helpful and remember to say your good mornings to your teacher and your classmates and not to fight or call names or use bad words, either. That's it, I think."

Chinese say Young Pioneers are like Scouts in the West, except that teachers and classmates decide who will belong. It has nothing to do now with parents' politics. To belong is a reward. Children say the kerchief is sacred to them and also it is useful— to fidget with or to nibble on in times of nervousness or boredom.

I have been a Young Pioneer for six years. Twice I have been to a big Young Pioneer congress. I was overjoyed. We sit very straight for the talks, because we are proud of ourselves. And other classmates who don't take part stand outside near the windows to look in at us. On some Sundays Young Pioneers have a picnic or go to the museum or help the weak and the sick.
Qifang "Kara" Wu

part of the city). China doesn't have housewives or househusbands. And so the center is open early and late. It welcomes children from the time they're fifty-six days old, and when it hasn't the space for them—it often hasn't—then grandparents or "hired grandparents" must serve as sitters.

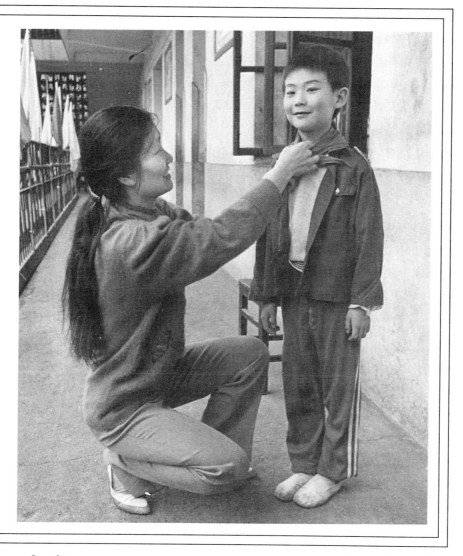

In this country, where grown-ups call each other "Comrade," youngsters at the center are taught to honor their red flag and to be ever kind, loyal, and helpful. They playact in little skits, wearing grown-up shoes and caps, taking turns at being Helpful Child, who picks up Farmer's spilled apples, who guides Old Man (hobble

hobble) across a street, who finds things for squinty Granny (she's lost her needle and her ration book).

Preschoolers are not invited to fingerpaint or to slosh at sinks or to haul blocks. Such messing about is not the custom, and the stories read aloud by teachers praise neatness and caution. When a storybook boy chases after a butterfly, he winds up not in a wonderland of adventure, but in a fierce stream, scared and wishing he'd stayed close to Grandpa.

This morning's last game before washup time, lunch, back rubs, and naps is the Farmer and the Sheep. Children are the Sheep. They run, *baa*-ing, some just laughing. At the count of ten they form a chain, holding each other around the waists or by shirttails. The teacher, who is Farmer, tries to snatch a sheep from the flock but may only take a loose one or a tag ender. Her snatching isn't easy, for the children twist quickly and shift direction.

This teacher says she likes the game for the running (she's fast on her feet) and for the lesson: Comrades together are protectors. Short of breath, she says it's the children's favorite game "because it's the wildest."

In China, twelve-year-olds, bogged down in homework and tests, already look back to the play of a lost childhood.

I remember child-care. At noon we must sleep, but we are playing and fighting on the beds. Our teacher is kind. When she tells us a story we become peaceful. In the afternoon we are chasing like tigers on the grass. Laughing. I remember my childhood forever.

Hong "Stacey" Shi

Reading Lessons

AT MAPLE MOUNTAIN Elementary, umbrellas hang from hooks at the back of the fourth-grade classroom. Here high windows let in good light. Riddles and poems fill the blackboards. A red banner up front spells out in large characters: "Love Our Motherland! Study with Diligence!" Sixty boys and girls, sitting straight, two to a bench, read aloud all together from their textbooks.

It's third period—language class. The teacher is on the move from aisle to aisle, her own book in hand. She reads aloud also, darting her eyes from face to face and back to the text again. Her voice is strong. At signals from her, a pupil stands to read solo or to repeat after her, in her tones, a hard sentence or new words. The child who bumbles is left standing while another is called on, and another, until the reading comes out right.

To read and write Chinese well takes a lifetime, but fourth graders, well on their way, are expected to know 2,000 of the 50,000 written Chinese characters. They'll need to know 3,000 by the time of their big exams to enter seventh grade, at least 4,000 to 5,000 by college.

Chinese children will tell a foreigner that Chinese is an easy language to speak. It has short words (one-syllable) and simple sentences, such as *chi bao la* (eat—full—already, to say "I have had enough to eat, thank you"). But Chinese is tremendously hard to write and to read. There's no alphabet, no twenty-six letters to help a person sound out s-p-o-t "spot," s-p-i-t "spit"; just thousands of picture words to memorize, one at a time, and most of them without a clue to help.

In this class there is a hush of concentration. And then there are sudden rushes of words, a din when the sixty voices are raised in a chorus. The teacher's pace is fast to keep heads from drooping, to keep thoughts from drifting off. She knows pupils were up before morning light. (Chinese are early risers.) Sometimes her pace is too fast. A girl loses her place on the page. A boy, also lost, slips his red kerchief up over his nose, bandit-style, hoping for a friend's laugh—which he doesn't get.

Today's reading sounds exciting. A foreign visitor to class can guess: This is a tale of adventure—it's about folk hero Monkey King in one of his seventy-two disguises. Or it's about Liberation Army soldiers swimming swift rivers. Not so. The guess is not even close.

Today's reading is about a committee. No madcap disguises or monkey somersaults through space. No daring swims. The committee came in the 1940s from Canada. It brought messages of respect and hope to the revolutionaries where they lived in far caves and struggled to become leaders of China.

So the electricity in today's air is from a plain bit of history. It's sparked by a lively teacher and quick kids and by the Chinese language, which is a puzzler and a challenge.

The shriek of a bell ends class. From thirty benches pupils jump to attention to shout good-byes to teacher Li. They stuff books, papers, and pencils into bookbags, then clatter downstairs and across the yard for the trip home to lunch and naps. It's raining, and parents, also on lunch break, have arrived with umbrellas and ponchos. (This is a city where changes of clothes are few. Families don't have washing machines or dryers, and laundry in the damp air stays wet Monday to Sunday. Children try not to get wet.)

As a foreign friend and teacher who wants to improve his Chinese, six-foot-tall American Alex rates a chair at the back of the classroom rather than a bench. Juggling his reader and two dictionaries on his lap, Alex says he keeps up, just barely, with his ten-year-old classmates. He shares homework chores with a boy from the back row who often falls behind too.

WATCH YOUR TONES
WHEN YOU SAY MA

If, speaking Chinese, you say you sat on a *ma*, which *ma* was it? You sat on your mother? Or on a horse, perhaps, or on a leech, an agate stone, or a grasshopper? On paper the meaning is clear, because each of these is a very different picture word. But each is pronounced "ma." And, speaking, you have only the tone of your voice to tell which *ma* you mean.

Chinese children, who hear the language all the time, scarcely need to think which tone to use. Foreigners get into tangles and must practice hard.

Consider: 1. In the flat tone (the way you'd say in English "Ma's here"), *ma* means mother in Chinese. 2. In a rising tone ("You home, Ma?"), *ma* means hemp or cord. 3. In a dipping tone—down and up again, sounding doubtful ("You *mean* it, Ma-a?"), *ma* means horse. 4. In a falling tone ("Look out, Ma!"), *ma* means curse. A hitch is: There are not enough tones to go around. The down-up *ma* can also mean leech or agate stone. The falling *ma* can be grasshopper. So guesses are still required. But if you sat on a third-tone *ma*, you've at least narrowed the field to horse, agate stone, or leech.

Consider also that *ma ma hu hu* (horse horse tiger tiger) is a good Chinese answer to "How are things?" when you want to say that things are not too bad and that you are muddling along.

Children who say Chinese is easy like to rattle off this jingle full of *mas*:

Ma¹-ma chi ma³	Mother rides the horse
Ma³ man	The horse is slow
Ma¹-ma ti ma³	Mother kicks the horse
Ma³ ti ma-ma¹	The horse kicks mother
Ma¹-ma ma⁴ ma³	Mother curses the horse

CHAPTER

＝ 3 ＝

Eye Exercises and Jump-Ups

IN CHINA eyes are used hard. Children at school write the picture-word characters, which are clusters of chicken-scratch dots and strokes. They write rows of them in small squares across sheets of paper, then read back again to check: did they put a stroke too few? or a stroke at a wrong slant? or a stroke without the hook it may need at its tip? Children stare at characters, printed small and close together, in books. Nighttimes they focus still, on homework.

To pamper the eyes and to strengthen them, schools declare twice-a-day time-outs for eye exercise, the same as in factories. Not all the Changsha children who need eyeglasses can afford to buy them. So help for ever better squinting power is appreciated.

Over intercoms—at the start of third period, again at fifth pe-

Students say the required eye exercises, mornings and afternoons, are both boring and restful.

riod—the step-by-step instructions crackle out loudly into the classrooms. The four exercises to be done sixty-four times each are set to music, and the volume is always high. (In China, *earstrain*, it seems, is not a worry.) Elbows on desks, boys and girls close their eyes. For five minutes they massage with their fingers—on the forehead, alongside the eyes, alongside the nostrils. They stroke across eyebrows and cheekbones.

In elementary school, teachers cruise the aisles to check. In middle school, monitors do it for them. (Monitors are honored students. They report on classmates' conduct and take attendance. They advise the teacher where to go on a class trip—to Moon Island—and what to do there—cook and eat.)

I don't like to do the exercises. Until the monitor comes up to me, my eyes are open and I look around. That's bad of me. But sometimes I do the exercises very carefully, for example when I meet a difficult problem or when I can't continue a composition. I do the exercises. And when I finish and open my eyes, I have an idea. Good! I have found a way.

Run liang "Rosemary" Qu

In school, everyday routines of jump-ups and toe touches out on the playground are required also. They're a welcome change after the indoor air and too much sitting on benches, side by side, sixty pupils and more to a classroom.

There's serious gym at school and serious exercise at home as well. Changsha boys and girls grow up knowing the body serves a person well and deserves the best training.

At home, young people are used to seeing parents and grandparents at their early-morning *tai chi* exercise. In a group or on their own, the adults flex ankles, wrists. They reach, like underwater swimmers, like skaters in slow slow motion, their faces emptied,

One "free spirit" throws wide her arms, happily out of step with her classmates.

Children at Maple Mountain Elementary enter into their follow-the-leader exercise routines—jumps and arm flings—with gusto.

it seems, smooth and untroubled. The ones who aren't at this soft form of exercise may be working out with weapons, bony old grannies among them, slashing the air with swords. Children hope to be like them, but most mornings they must copy word lists and check math in their scramble toward school.

On a Sunday I get up early and do exercises outside. The air is fresh and cool. I breathe it and close my eyes. The sky is not bright, but threads in it tell me the sun comes out soon. This is morning. In China we say it gives us vigor and makes our minds clear.

Lien "Jessica" Fei

Some schools offer early training in the skills of *wushu*. Chinese people always wish to explain that *wushu*, or martial arts, got its start as maneuvers for combat, but that it has nothing to do with getting sore at people and beating them up. In this city, famous for its *wushu*, children who learn the basics are proud.

Exercise—with style—is a daily part of schoolwork for Chinese pupils, who go to school six days a week.

Please stand straight, then use your hands to touch the ground. Your legs must still be straight. This is a beginner thing in wushu, *martial arts. If you're good at* wushu, *you will feel comfortable. Illness is not able to go with you. You will never fear others fighting you. Though your enemies are many, you can easily do with them.*

Remember, you practice wushu *to make yourself strong and to protect yourself and to help weakers. If you practice it for fighting, you must never be successful. Practicing* wushu *isn't easy. It takes suffering.*

Kai "Samuel" Jiang

Brush Painting

IN ART CLASS, Tang Yen, thirteen, works fast and with great concentration—to paint his eagles, soaring. He uses black ink, a puddle of it on a plate, and makes shades of gray by thinning the ink with water. The wide brush is for his slashing big strokes and for his washes of gray. The narrow brush is for sharp bits of detail such as the birds' claws. Working fast is important, and so is the looseness that comes with practice. This young artist has painted a lot of eagles.

Tang Yen knows the Chinese saying "Ink sings and the brush dances." He wants his birds to fly and to show power and grace also. And then—disappointment! This painting, *he* says, is not good. "The legs are too large by far."

He does a new picture and is pleased. His teacher understands.
He too is pleased. At the edge the boy signs his name and writes
"The eagle hits the sky with his wing."

Artwork is for everyone. Tang Yen did his first in primary school
and liked it from the start. Now, in middle school, he also likes
math and music and English and soccer. On his own he has taken
to sketching with pen and ink—scenes of people on the street
selling red peppers, Popsicles, and candied apples, also youngsters
climbing onto a crowded bus.

For his two American teachers, who call him Christopher, he
doodles. It was their idea—to get him past feeling that every picture
must be perfect. For them he turns out crookedy creatures and
scenes from *Star Wars*.

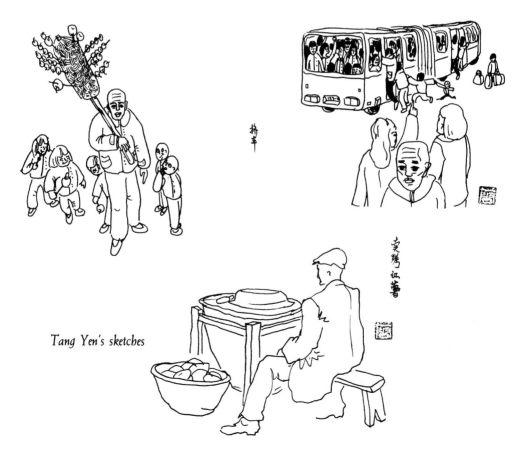

Tang Yen's sketches

English in School

THE CHILDREN who take the class in English conversation, taught by Americans Alex and Heidi, are learning to speak out in strange-sounding ways, never mind the mistakes, which are often real howlers. They are learning to laugh and be laughed at, and to keep speaking. They're willing and excited.

English, the language of cowboys and cartoon characters, is enormously popular. It's important on exams to get into college. Parents try hard to get children into classes such as these at the Ya-li Middle School, which have native speakers.

Children work hard to do well. They're quick to pick up songs and jingles and slang—how to use "chill out" and "nerd" and to stick Kick Me signs on a friend's back. They repeat Mother Goose,

Pupils in Alex's conversation class hope to be asked: What's that on your plate? As fans of Dr. Seuss nonsense books, they reply, "Green eggs and ham, thank you!" They also want to be asked: Are you sure? so they can shoot back at a near shout: "Ab-so-lute-ly." It's a favorite word.

loud, louder, wanting their Jack Sprat, their Jack and Jill, to be word perfect. ("Alex, Alex, what's 'off did trot,' what does it mean?") Boys and girls ask for Western names and say: Call me Paul . . . Walter . . . Colleen. Wen becomes Wendy; Jie, Jenny. These pupils wish to bob for apples and carve pumpkins in October. They like puzzling out proverbs on the board (HASTE MAKES WASTE) and proverb mix-ups (WAY A THERE'S WILL A THERE'S WHERE).

The American teachers rate a special privilege—to teach small classes and sit in a circle with their pupils. In a morning class with Alex, talk is about The Future—not the children's future, though boys and girls sometimes talk about that also. (When they do, they roll their eyes and play dead, zapped by the years of study and by the scariest exams yet to come.) Talk is about the future tense. In Chinese a person says: I yesterday go. I tomorrow go. No change in the "go." So Chinese children must learn in English to say: I will go tomorrow.

Alex puts a question: "If suddenly in Changsha all the bicycles turn into cars, what then? Tell what will happen and use 'will' in your answers."

"If bikes turn into cars, the streets will be jammed." "People will be late for work." "There will be accidents." "Repairs will cost too much." "The government will sell the cars to foreign countries." "People will be glad to ride bikes again."

Another "What Will Happen": What will happen if Chinese people no longer eat rice? "People will try bread and butter." "They will get fat." "People will get a awful feeling."

Both American teachers like the reading book they use. They like the people in it, especially Barney—nice and funny—who's a cab driver and a mechanic, smart, good at his work, pleased. The teachers like the message, because service and fix-it work, such as Barney's, are pretty much scorned in China. Parents wish desk jobs for their children.

At the board, Heidi, chalk in hand, sketches out in quick strokes Barney's cab. The pupils give her the words, and she letters onto it: SPEEDY CAB COMPANY. "What's another word for 'speedy'? Yes, 'fast.' Barney's a speedy driver, a fast driver. What else? Yes, he's an excellent driver. And how does he feel about his work? Right, he enjoys it because . . . sure, because he meets interesting people on the job. What else is there about Barney? Of course. He's friendly. Frank, are you?"

CHOOSE A CHINESE NAME

In the Ya-li class list, some names are patriotic. A girl is Hong, meaning Red. Boys are Jun (Army) and Li-jun (Victorious Army). In English class and often on the playground, these students call each other Harriet and Jerry and Lincoln, using the names invented for them by their teacher.

Other names are romantic or inspiring:

Long-fei (Flying Dragon)	Francis
Shan (Mountain)	Sean
Lin-ye (Forest Leaf), nickname Lin-yezzi	Linda
Yen (Smoke)	John
Feng-quang (Wide Wind or Glorious View)	Fred
Ming-ding (Bright Power)	Michael
Yu-ming (Jade Bright)	Julia
Hai-jiang (Rising Sea)	Harold
Ming-chien (Bright Spring; for a boy also)	Melanie
Jing-feng (Strong Wind)	Janet
Hai-yan (Sea Swallow)	Hilary
Lei (Thunder)	Kate

Some names are given for the sound of them: Ling-ling (the ring of a bell), Tao-tao (the splash of waves), Fang-fang (fragrance). One mother named her children Lin, Bin, and Jin for the rhyme. She started with Lin, meaning forest (the picture word is two side-by-side trees). "I wanted my daughter to be straight and true, not to bend or be devious."

"Yes," says Frank. "I am very friendly."

As she talks, Heidi strikes her chalk against the board, adding streaks of light from the headlights. "While Barney drives, he often talks to passengers." Heidi mugs out how Barney gabs over his shoulder. She adds stars and moon. (All of her drawing, she says, is to encourage pupils to doodle and scratch their own notions onto paper in a playful manner.)

"What might Barney say?" She draws a big balloon over the taxi and fills it with Pearl's comment. Pearl says: "It is a nice night." The teacher writes: NICE NIGHT, ISN'T IT?

Pupils are surprised by the breezy manner of American teacher Heidi. But they see she is serious about her teaching and she wishes them to be frank and open with her. "We talk about our lives and the world. We must think where we stand on things."

"I AM BRAVE"

Stars from the English conversation class brighten an afternoon with their play for an adored old teacher, who once was a chopsticks-snatching prankster and the school's soccer captain. The children's play isn't so much show business as it is a chance to exercise their English and offer it as a gift of love.

Milling about outdoors until curtain time, members of the cast repeat favorite lines: "Guard, take her to the forest!" "I will, my Queen." Or they introduce themselves to foreign guests, who mill about also. "I am Walter," says one actor, bright-eyed and excited. In careful English he adds, "I am Sleepy." His remark makes better sense as his friends speak up after him: "I'm Dopey," "I'm Bashful," "I'm Doc," and on through the seven dwarfs.

"My name is Pearl. I speak English badly," says the guard. (She's wrong about that.) "But I am brave."

Owl spreads her wings, Mirror holds up her shining square. Guard tips her hat, as members of the *Snow White* cast line up for their photograph.

CHAPTER

⌐ 6 ¬

Children's Palace Night

AT THE CHILDREN'S Palace, backstage before curtain time, excited-looking boys and girls in costume jostle and chase each other. This *is* show business, with footlights and a packed auditorium. The young performers stand still just long enough to accept good wishes from grown-ups and to tip up faces for rouge, eyeliner, and last-minute dustings of powder. These are boys and girls who've shown special talent and been invited to take after-school classes in music and in dance. They've already won three big competitions. At tonight's show they get their medals.

Every seat in the house is filled. Parents are here, friends, teachers, neighbors—a good audience. From the start to the end of the program, the crowd is enthusiastic—but not quiet. People move

Untroubled by the footlights, "Three Hairs," age three, plays his violin, watched by his family in the wings.

about, greet each other, talk, especially, it seems, through parts they like best. And Donald Duck Popsicles are licked in time to the music.

The youngest performer is a violinist in knee socks. He's three, and Three Hairs is his nickname. He's a crowd pleaser. So are a trio of saucy dancers in sailor suits. The biggest hand goes to the lineup of sixty children receiving the medals, which are hung about their necks on wide ribbons.

It's after ten when families stream out from the bright theater. Children with painted cheeks are holding hands with grown-ups. They are still jigging little dance steps. The streets are dark. Under a lamp hung from a tree, one ten-year-old sings a last song to his parents.

Nervous? Parents say child performers don't know what nervous means. Children practice and compete and from youngest times they sing, dance, and recite. Whoever steps through the door at home—aunt, neighbor, friend—is their audience. A stage is fun for them.

PRACTICE MAKES PERFECT

Gold-medalist Man-jiang is the kind of boy who ducks behind a parent when he's asked a question and pops out again once he's figured an answer. He's bright and he's shy. (His name means Slow-Flowing River.) It was his shyness, from when he used to whisper, that led to singing lessons. And songs set Man-jiang free. He sings in a good strong voice, gladly and often—folk songs, patriotic songs, romantic songs ("The Herdsman and His Flute"). He may not answer a request instantly, but he'll knock on a door the next morning and pour out the asked-for song. Every day Man-jiang practices violin with his mother as coach and his father as audience. (The boy's father says he never listened to music until the boy played for him.)

As for his medal won at the Children's Palace, Man-jiang kept it on his pillow the first night. He bit it to see if it was chocolate, he sang and talked to it until his parents yelled at him: Be quiet! Since then he keeps the medal in their bedroom in a locked cupboard, inside a drawer, in the box with the family's identity cards and food coupons.

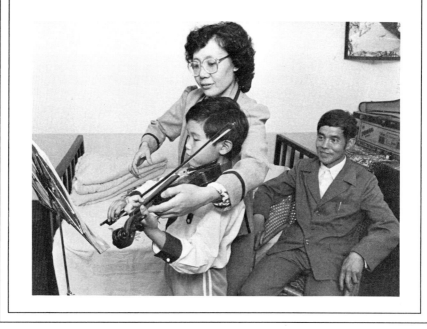

CHAPTER

7

Puppets, Wigs, Wushu

THROUGH THE BIG old building of the High School for Performing Arts there's an air of excitement. There's a clattering of feet up and down the wood stairs, and—as doors open and close—bursts of orchestra music, of song, of *clack-clack-clacks* giving a beat. Students in T-shirts and cotton pants rush by carrying crowns, wigs, and filmy costumes.

It's an honor to study here, to learn China's age-old shadow plays and its operas. Students from all parts of the province are chosen for their talent and good character. They live at the school and are kept tumbling and breathless. For Chinese theater is a mix of dance, song, martial arts, acting, orchestra, and acrobatics. These teenagers have a mix of skills to master.

41

Behind the screen, students (with sticks held to puppets' heads, shoulders, hips) "walk" their puppets in ways to express moods.

Along the way they must learn the strong traditions for the music (mostly loud to raucous), for the costumes (elaborate), and the makeup (red face for a loyal man at court, white nose for a clown, black furrows on brow and cheek for a warrior). People in an audience will know the stories, know the fights and love duets to come. They'll await this jealous look, that slash, and will thrill to see it done beautifully.

Success at the school leads to jobs with a troupe, perhaps to a lifetime on stage and to travel, even far beyond Changsha. The students hope for such good luck. Life for them is exhausting—to keep up with math, with everyday high school work, along with their performing. But students say that ordinary school, if they had to drop back, would be a bore to them.

In a first-floor classroom, the lesson is on Chinese shadow puppets: how to "walk" them across a white screen. In a theater, with strong lights from behind, the audience will see only the puppets—in glowing color and sharp outline—not the boys and girls moving them.

The teacher is an actress with a melodious strong voice. She is well known for her roles in opera as birds—as a crane or a mythical phoenix. For her students she beats out rhythms with hollow bamboo blocks and asks the students to show her, by how they move the puppets, first the brisk walk of a warrior, then the creaky walk of an old-timer, then someone who is happy (the teacher's blocks go *clickclicketyclick*), and someone who is (*clackclack*) mad.

In a sunny upstairs room, second-year students (sixteen- and seventeen-year-olds) work with large marionettes held above their heads. They move the puppets in smooth dance steps across the floor to music, using the right hand to support the tall paper-wire-wood body and to control the head, the left hand to control the arms. An audience won't see these performers either—only the glides and twirls of the marionettes.

In the largest room, big as a gym, a boy and girl practice, many times over, a martial-arts routine. They practice silently and with the orchestra—a din of cymbals, gongs, drums, flutes, two-stringed violins. They work until the energy is high and the footwork is fast. The stares, the footstamps, and the shouts between boy and girl must all be fierce enough to please the performers, and their two instructors also.

The boy, who begins with two sabers, loses the saber from his

Sixteen-year-olds, manipulating marionettes, glide through the moves of a female lead in
The Dream of the Red Chamber.

right hand and he somersaults away to safety. The girl somersaults, holding her weapon and his, throwing his to him. He stamps, he shouts, then he bounds back to continue the fight. (Students are reminded that fight styles differ with the weapons. Curved sabers must show the rush and pounce of a tiger. A straight sword cuts the air in birdlike fashion. Bamboo poles have a flex to them for the twists and lunges of a dragon. It's poor form to mix the styles of fighting.)

Members of the orchestra cannot now ponder birds, tigers, dragons. They are called on to rehearse singers in a love duet from *Flower Drum Song*, and they must shift their mood quickly from shrill and rackety to dreamlike.

Members of the student orchestra play through rehearsals of martial arts routines and operas.

CHAPTER

8

Shaves and Haircuts

Every morning at six fifty I walk to the school. In winter I walk quickly with my hands in my pockets. It's cold and the wind blows. I have on a lot of clothes and move my legs faster and faster. I don't have a mood to see what happens around me. But in spring, in fall, a warm wind blows me warm and I see around myself—the trees, the people. I walk slowly in summer or I will be too hot. I sing in a low voice. Always I see the buses run more slowly than I walk. With friends on the way to school I speak jokes. I think what I should do in the noon and in the evening after my homework. I think, will my mother let me watch television?

Fei "Eric" Ming

IN CHANGSHA, where streets serve as front porches and workshops, boys and girls scuffing along toward school see people at a dozen

46

Top: *A carpenter and his apprentice, working by the side of the road, josh with passersby.*

Left: *A noodlemaker wants sunshine for his noodles drying on sidewalk racks.*

occupations. By lunchtime, at home, they've looked at a hundred things for sale along the curbs. In the course of an afternoon's trips, scarcely straying from their track, they've hovered at the edges of ten thousand small happenings—of selling, fixing, building.

Nothing out of the ordinary, they say. Though with such chances to stop and look, city kids do well to reach school or home again without parents setting out to search.

For boys and girls living on Yellow Earth Hill, the route is never dull. It starts them out past farms and along the busy Ling Road. It leads them through green plots where farmers tie up vines and slosh buckets of smelly stuff over their plants, and frogs croak greetings from the ditches. At the far corner, on a morning in June, the shutters are still shut at the office of the doctor, but across from the Number Four bus stop a carpenter—his shop open, front and back—is planing away at wood window frames. He's ankle-deep in shavings.

Other carpenters in the next block put the finishing touches to a bed. They've set it up on the sidewalk, and from peg to peg of the wood frame they crisscross hemp to make the padding. Next door a pair of blacksmiths in a hole-in-the-wall smithy pound in turns on a red-hot rod, sparks flying. They shout to each other and, between whangs, stop for rests to puff and mop brows.

The noodlemaker is an old fellow in a blue "Mao" jacket such as everyone wore fifteen years ago. (Then it was practically a uniform. Now no one much wears it. Clothes are quirkier and more colorful.) He's a fusspot, this noodle man. And he mutters over his fringes of dough that hang outdoors on frames. "Aiya!" Will they ever dry if this day, like the four before it, is clammy and stays damp? When the street sweeper sweeps by, he shrugs. Her stirring up a cloud of grit won't help the noodles either.

On a side lane, farmers have set out trays and tubs of food in front of the squashed-together small houses. The egg lady has arrived. She looks fresh and full of pep, even though she's walked since before dawn from the countryside, carrying her baskets.

Boys and girls passing through, shouldering their bookbags, must choose—to dart on by or to listen in on haggles over prices, or to hang about by a card game or maybe by a construction site watching cement hauled in buckets. Just one run across the lane to inspect pigs' ears and they've missed the eel man. He's snatched up a handful of wrigglers from his frothed-up tub and made a sale of them. (So fresh! he says. Pulled from their holes in the rice-paddy mud this morning.)

Just an instant's look at the locksmith or the shoe repairman at the curb, stitching, and these watchers find they must put on a burst of speed. Or once again they'll reach school out of breath, only seconds before the bell.

Children are in luck who pass the really big markets on their route. They hear the banter where ten sellers in a row weigh out their eggs, where fifteen have tubs of eels, all in noisy competition. Such a market has peppers in rainbow colors—heaps and mounds of them—radiantly shining. Cabbages, beans, mushrooms, melons also. Stockings, peanuts. Roots, teas, and transparent bean noodles. Chickens. Turtles.

Sometimes there's the racket and smoke of firecrackers when a new shop celebrates its opening. Always there's street food to watch in the making—fragrant soups and snacks. *Shaobing* are biscuits with sprinkles of sesame seed, baked on oil drum stoves. *Yutiao* are long golden twists of doughnutty dough, fried in vats of hot, spitting oil. (The doughnut treats are delicious when hot and fresh. They're awful when they are old, which is why *yutiao* is also the name for tough old gentlemen.)

Afternoons, a riverside lane is an inviting, quiet place. The sidewalk mops shop, with mops made of bright-colored strips of cloth, gives it a festive look. So does the family wash. It hangs high—sweat suits, rags, babies' slit-seat pants—where a long-handled hook is needed to reach it down again.

The lane is filled with people. Some live here, some work here. Some shop here or, like the children returning to school yawning from naps, they just wish to thread their way through. People pushing bikes or pulling carts make slow progress.

Grannies sit in chairs well out into the traffic. They're winding wool or knitting. They bathe a tot in a wood tub, or they mind a little counter of teas for sale by the glass, or sometimes oranges, bananas, bottles of pop.

The bicycle repairman has left his dark, cluttered shop for the street, where he treats a wheel for busted spokes. The umbrella repairman has spokes of his own to mend. He carries tools and spare parts in baskets hung from his shoulders, and he sets down his load, to work, wherever he finds a customer.

In a shed where chips of coal are being pressed into bricks for cooking with, shovels scrape and a machine splutters. The workers are smudged with black on clothes and skin.

At the end of the lane, a young barber has set up shop on a

flight of steps. His tilt-back chair and his basins are at the broadest place of the stairs. His tin-can stove with the steaming kettle is one step up. He has lathered his customer in hot suds and is shaving him from the top of his head to his collarbone.

Onlookers find they agree: The barber's work is well done. Street sweepers sweeping past, though, say loud enough to be heard: Some old turnip must have cash to throw away if he spends it on a shave. They get a half grin from the customer, who rubs a hand across the back of his neck and looks well satisfied.

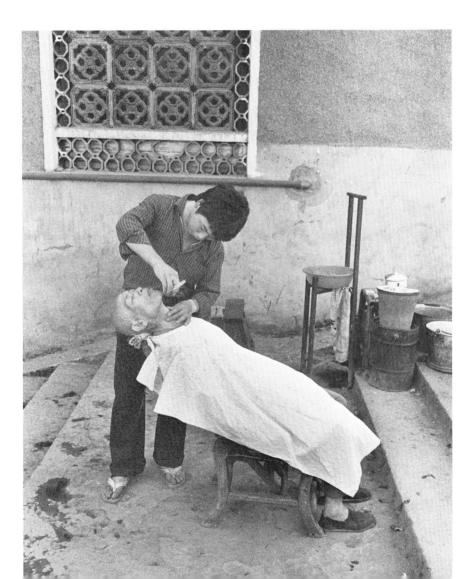

Kids, at the top of the steps, turn onto the big posh Wu Yi Boulevard (the name means Five One, or Fifth Month First Day—to honor a workers' holiday on May First). They quicken their pace in the fast traffic. Haircuts for boys and girls are swift work, done by a parent. Haircuts are free at home.

C H A P T E R

9

The Doctor Is In

BY THE NUMBER Four bus stop, just beyond his open door, the doctor massages a patient's large purple bruise. Then he gently taps it with a small glass hammer and applies a warm tealike tincture and dressings. The patient goes from nervous whimperings to hiccups to brave smiles. She says she's grateful. The doctor nods thoughtfully. His solemn gaze and his eyeglasses, sliding down his nose, give him the look of a friendly cousin—reassuring.

Small girls and boys standing in his doorway know to watch in respectful silence and to lick their Popsicles very quietly. They make room up front for shorter children.

When the doorway is filled, there is always the window around the side to watch through. Or there's the doctor's young helper to

talk to when he arrives with leaves, roots, barks, and flowers to be dried for medicines. (Many ingredients for the medicine packets can be gathered in the city. Ground-up elk antlers and such may need to be bought.)

For another patient, with a painful thumb, the doctor applies heat from a kind of cigar of paper soaked with herbs. Heat from the glowing "cigar" reaches the skin through a thin slice of fresh ginger root, which he holds to the patient's trouble spot.

Both patients are also treated with pricks from acupuncture needles (stuck in at the second joints of the middle fingers). The needles are slender as hairs, and they help to regulate the body's flow of energy, or *qi* (pronounced "chee").

This doctor works in a tiny office where his "waiting room" is a three-seater bench in arm's reach of his desk. He is the fourth-generation healer in his family. He's not been to medical school but has learned his traditional Chinese medicine at home, from wide reading and a lifetime of study. He has good results, he says, even with victims of snakebite.

His use of herbs and acupuncture exists side by side in China with Western-style medicine. Many people use a mix. Children get Western-style checkups with tests and shots. For coughs or flu or aches, the family may rely on packets and advice from a genial, skilled doctor like this one at the Number Four bus stop.

CHAPTER

10

Bikes and Buses

A BICYCLE means transportation and independence. It's a happy *zai jian* ("good-bye") to cram-jammed city buses where waits are long and the squash is ferocious and scary.

On a bike there's the thrill of mornings in a stream of traffic, pedaling in a glitter of spokes, a blur of white blouses, and white shirts. The main drag, Wu Yi Boulevard, has lanes for buses and for cars, other lanes for bikes. The Wu Yi has cops also, presiding over traffic circles.

Elsewhere for riders it's: Keep your wits about you. Steer clear of jeeps and carts and ancient trucks that break down. Be on the lookout for the dreamers, and for crazies who dart across a path, and for joggers with baskets of chickens hung from carrying poles.

Favorite makes of bicycle are Forever and Phoenix and the Flying Pigeon, which cost two months and more of a parent's pay. Less classy makes are cheaper. So are secondhand bikes, though even they cost a month's pay and then some.

A bicycle in the city must be equipped with a license, a good lock, brakes, and a bell—the bigger the bell the better. No one wears a helmet. No one has lights either, even though streets are mostly dark at night with only a lamp or two per block hung from the trees.

Night biking, when traffic is thin, can be a pleasure. But it's nervous making also, for great potholes and ditches appear without warning. Drop-offs are unmarked.

By about age nine, some Changsha children ride bikes to school. By thirteen, more than half are riding. Bikes, in a society without private cars, are also much used to carry loads. They're the family car and the company van. Out on the streets, bicycles can be seen piled high with crates, sacks, stacks of newspaper, whole shipments of brooms. The owner walks alongside keeping the load in balance.

The History of My Bike.

I have a beautiful bike. His name is Forever. His hometown is the Shanghai Bicycle Factory. He is painted with black. He looks like a black treasure. Also some of him is bright, just like a mirror. When he is in the sun, he is dazzling.

The bike is a gift from my uncle. When he knew that I became a student of Ya-li Middle School, he gave the new bike to me as a present. How happy I am, because school is not near to my home and I hate to take the bus.

I often ride very fast because I get up late. One bad day I'm not in luck. My key is lost and I must take five minutes to look for it. After that I want my bike to go in the shortest time. But to my surprise the bike looks sick. He can't go quickly. He can't go even as quickly as an old slow bus. So I am late and the teacher orders me to clean the classroom.

Right: *Children fear the squash in crowded buses.*

Bottom: *Bike traffic on the big Wu Yi Lu is fast but orderly.*

Sometimes I repair my bike myself. But I'm a not very good repairman. He becomes worse and worse. So I have to call my father for help. Sometimes also I'm a not careful rider. One day riding home, I saw a beautiful Mitsubishi car. I looked at it for a long time. And, Ping! I hit a Isuzu truck and fell to the ground. I picked up the bike very quickly because I saw a man come towards me. I rode very quickly and heard: Hi! Stop the child! I was not to pay attention to him, and I tried my best to get home. I was very satisfied with my speed. It was not the bike's fault—my fall—but a mistake I made.

Now I have ridden my bike for two years. He became older and not as beautiful as when he was new. But I still like him because he is one of my best friends.

Ming "Benjamin" Luo

(NOTE: Chinese don't use words for "he," "she," "it"; hence they are apt to say in English "My brother, she is busy," and Benjamin says "My bike, he is beautiful.")

In Changsha heavy traffic is a fact of life. And children, who must brave it, talk a lot about the accidents they see and the fear in their hearts over rude pileups inside buses.

If you want to ride on a bus, you must have a big power. People stand with no room between. You must sway, like fish. If on the way you fall, the other persons must land on top of you.

Man "Laura" Luo

CHAPTER

11

Father, Son, and Old Duck Tang

QUAN is on time for supper. Mostly he's not. Nine years old, he's a runabout, a bright dreamer. Mornings, when he dawdles, his father must often ride him to school by bicycle. Suppertimes he's slipped away to play in some corner of the compound. He's watching a pickup soccer game out by the compound's kitchens—teenagers kicking the ball around, trying to keep from kicking it into the coal pile. Or he and his friends are racing around the bricks of a building project, or sitting on steps, talking. And the father is out again by bike to fetch him.

Quan is home promptly on Sundays because it's *Donald Duck* night—his treat of the week. And a friend is invited to watch with him. Sundays all across vast China, the streets are empty of youngsters between six thirty and seven. Like Quan and friend, they're in front of a television screen, laughing at a duck. They call him Tang Lao Ya ("Old Duck Tang").

For Quan the fun ends too soon. Even with an extra half hour of *Captain Black Cat*, the number-two cartoon favorite, it's hard to wave good-bye to his friend and settle down to a mop-up of homework. The boy stalls. He skids his missile launcher around the floor. It's a chunk of Styrofoam with nails he poked into it for missiles.

At eight the boy's mother must leave, bicycling out to the hospital where she puts together herb medicines. Quan's father has plunged into his own pile of paperwork. And Quan bravely follows his example.

Television is a double pleasure when a friend comes to share it. The friend's apartment is the same as Quan's—three rooms, cement floors, spare furnishings, a calendar. A hallway telephone serves the building.

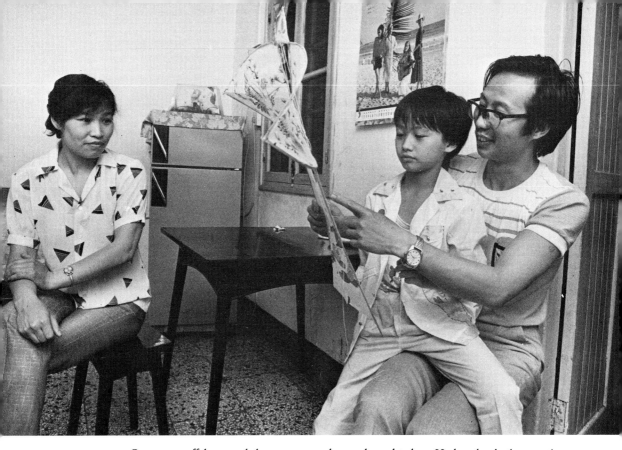

Quan puts off homework by inspecting the patch on his kite. He bought the kite on the street with money from his parents.

He does the fill-in-the-blank questions first. They're easy but sometimes there's a trick to them. Math problems next. They're hard—about kilograms of seeds and tons of cement. On little runs into the living room, the boy suggests to his father a story, please, or a quick game of cards or chess. He's shooed back to work, as expected.

The new word list could be worse. Quan copies the characters until he figures he has a good grip on them. The real trouble with the reading assigned for Monday is the questions at the end of it. They need to be answered in writing. (How *does* the honey locust tree in the school yard help children in every season?)

More than once the boy pops out from the bedroom where he works, looking again for comfort and bits of talk. ("In America, do they also have too much homework?" "Yes, of course they do.") Then Quan writes, erasing a lot and patching: The tree keeps off rain. It gives shade to play under. Seeds from the tree—you boil them up—wash away spots of ink. Dry leaves burn and give warmth.

The job is done. At heart the father sides with his yawning son. The work *is* long and it's tedious. There may be playful ways to learn, but school in China is not kind to dreamers. By the time a bright runabout child really wants to study hard, he may find he's lost the chance.

Even very young children must do well on exams. It's the way to get from sixth grade into a key middle school with the extra help there to do well on exams all over again. Flunk at ninth grade, and it's the end of schooldays. It's the start of a worrisome long wait to be assigned (who knows where) to make change, perhaps, behind a counter or to haul loads or to be a soldier. And the work—like it or not—may be for life.

Quan is a puzzle to his father, who hopes for more years of study for Quan and more chance to find what he will do and become. In the father's own life, school opened new worlds and freed him from the bleak toil of his ancestors. He was the first ever in his family to read. Now he teaches over the radio. At night he writes.

The father's peasant background, his big family, his woodchopping chores from childhood, are all close to his heart. He knows they made him proud and strong. That's why he named Quan for the clear spring in the farm village. The boy has happily heard the story ten thousand times: that a beggar was given a drink from the

spring, and ever after, it ran warm in winter and surprisingly cool in summer. Two swallows and a dragon, underground, guard the spring always. The story came from the father's mother. It was the only story she knew to tell. Her life was hard.

The name gives Quan a good feeling. So does his father's name, which means Riches and Happiness. The "riches" part is a family joke. But Quan likes to hear his father say that he did after all get the wish his farm family wished for him, though it's not cash. His rich happiness, the father says, is to read and to write. *And* it's to chase after "a son with nothing on his mind but a duck."

The use of his father's desk helps Quan to stick with his schoolwork, which takes him until ten and after every night to finish. His father says the boy knows some 1,500 Chinese characters.

CHAPTER

⌐ 12 ⌐

To Cook Is "Hot and Dangerous"

CHANGSHA FOLK are proud cooks. Though some now use gas stoves, many more must still mess about with the coal. They either buy coal bricks or they make them, stamping them out from a mix of powdered coal and mud. Cooks place two such bricks in a metal-drum stove with a pan on top, and they light bits of wood underneath. The hope is always that the bricks will burn clean and not smoke up the apartment.

Such a stove is slow to fire up and a bother to shut down again, which must be done because half-used bricks are taken out and saved to be used again. The smoke and bother of it, and the fact that water runs cold from the tap, is why thermos bottles are household items. People use the thermoses to store up quantities of scalding water. Then they have it for washups and for the cups

A city-farm kitchen has a supply of coal bricks (far right) to cook with. One family is apt to use four or five in a day.

Breakfast cooks at a compound kitchen.

of tea that are forever sipped and passed about and pressed into the hands of friends at the start of conversations.

Bothersome stoves are also a reason to run out to the cafeteria (there's one in every neighborhood) and to turn in coupons for carryouts. Early mornings, a stream of neighbors, dressed for offices and for school, pours out from such a kitchen. They're exchanging how-do-you-dos. They're saying, *"Ni hao"* ("You fine?") or *"Chi guo fan la"* (literally "Have you eaten?" but just a polite greeting also). They're carrying pans of food, still steaming—soups, puffy buns, some plain, some with meat or sweets.

At home, breakfast is mostly leftovers. Or it's a hot runny rice cereal with Changsha's famous chopped turnip pickles for trimmings. Lunch or supper is apt to be a rice dish or a noodle dish with the vegetables (and the meat or chicken or fish, if any) cut into bite-size pieces and stir-fried quickly over high heat. The small pieces make a great sizzle as they hit the pan and send out explosive little *pop pop pops* and a cloud of smoke.

My mother and father only have one child—me. The work is not too much. So they didn't teach me anything to cook. But this summer holiday I went to my hometown, Shanghai, to meet my grandma and uncles. My grandma is an old, short woman, and I often helped her, so she taught me. I did always think cooking is an interesting work. It is not. It is an awful work. It is very hot and dangerous. I'm afraid to have a big fire. But now I can cook jiaozi *[dumplings], and fish with ginger and vinegar, and other things also. I think I can be a good cooker.*

Jin "Sharon" Wang

One serving dish is a usual family meal. It's cooked, some families say, by whichever parent comes home first. So it should be, for the

City-farm families beat the summer heat by eating supper outdoors.

PROFESSOR DRAGON'S BANQUET

Sunday noon, the family of Professor Dragon celebrates her coming home. She's been away, homesick, telling strangers about her children, about Martyrs' Park (where she planted trees as a school kid), about Changsha turnips, pickled to perfection. In America she ate American food politely, although she was not used to dairy products and to such a lot of bread. Chinese don't have much of either one at home. They're suspicious of cottage cheese ("peculiar"), though they find ice cream delicious.

Over lunch, the talk is noisy, in fits and starts, with many conversations at once. Chopsticks fly across the table to the serving dishes, with more trips to the fried potatoes than to anything else, even the fine fish. "In America potatoes are so big," says the professor. "You couldn't call them 'beans of the earth,' the way we call ours."

"China has some big potatoes too," says her son-in-law.

"No, I mean huge. You could make a meal of one."

"Yes, huge." The son-in-law once lived in a faraway province where potatoes are not bean size either. "Big as boots, they are. I've seen them."

The family drinks a toast to homecomings and to potatoes, the bigger the better.

modern slogan, "Women hold up half the sky," means that women are to share equally in schools and in jobs and (though it often doesn't happen) that men are to share in kitchen work. For a banquet on a special occasion, the center of the table is filled with serving dishes, piled high and decorated with raw turnips carved into cranes and cocks. For a banquet in Changsha, many of the dishes will be spicy hot. There will be stir-fried pork and red chili peppers, a whole steamed fish, shrimp, squid, and chicken prepared in maybe three different fashions, maybe even a platter of deep-fried chicken feet. There will be bean curd in a garlic sauce, and beef with floppy tree-ear mushrooms, and—last, not first—a delicate lotus-seed soup, only this time the mushrooms are silver ears.

Banquets often also include "thousand-year" eggs, served up like hard-boileds, only here the yokes are green and the jellied whites have turned translucent and the color of very strong tea. The eggs are not as old as their name, though it takes a month or so in a lime-mud pack to age them properly. Changsha school kids, who shriek with laughter over the Dr. Seuss book *Green Eggs and Ham*, must know that foreigners are surprised by a first look at such thousand-year eggs. To appreciate them takes a little practice.

13

Chopsticks with Chen-chen

CHEN-CHEN WEARS a purple hair bow and polish on her nails. She considers herself a friend to Mickey Mouse and talks to his big cutout, on the wall by her pillow. She is two years old. At school she eats with a spoon. Here at home she's invited to try grown-up tools. She will eat Sunday-morning breakfast with chopsticks.

This breakfast is tricky, because it's noodle soup and a fried egg. And both are slippery.

Chen-chen is nimble-fingered and confident. Her name, after all, means Morning. She was born at five A.M., at the close of the Hours of the Tiger, giving her courage, and at the start of the Hours of the Rabbit, giving her luck. Her birth year was the Year of the Ox, which, as any Chinese knows, inspires her to be bright, happy, and patient.

The noodles do slip. Batches one and two, nicely captured on the sticks, slip off again. Batch three makes a good start, till— *splat!*—it slips also, and not this time back into the broth but onto the tabletop. The fourth try is a winner. Then it is Contact! and Lift! three more times. The noodles are delivered to the mouth, and all the dangly noodle ends are neatly tapped in, between the lips, by the tip ends of the chopsticks. (Chopsticks are intended to deliver the food, not, as a spoon does, to enter the mouth with it.)

It makes sense for Chen-chen, and it's good manners, to hold the bowl up close to her face and drink the broth neatly from the rim. It's good manners also to shovel in the last noodle bits in a

series of quick strokes. Shoveling, complete with little slurps, is fine form with chopsticks.

The fried egg, a Western kind of egg, requires some study. How to cope with it? It's as big around as a saucer. Chen-chen's tactic is to choke up with her fingers on the sticks closer to the tips. Her eyes say: This grip may not be proper. The set of her chin says: I bet it works. It does, and a satisfied youngster downs her egg and accepts her family's congratulations.

Teenagers say it feels to them as if they've used chopsticks always. They can't remember learning, though slick foods such as sea cucumbers, sea slugs, and slices of mushroom are still a challenge.

ANIMAL SIGNS:
ARE YOU A BRIGHT OX?

Is yours the Year of the bright Ox or the talented Rabbit? To find the animal signs for birth years before 1976, add 12 to your birth year (or add as many twelves as you need) in order to reach a date on the chart. Thus, for Chen-chen's friend Mickey Mouse, "born" in 1928, it takes four twelves to bring him to 1976—by the chart, a Year of the Dragon. Among Chinese, Dragon years are favorites. And August 8 in the Year of the Dragon 1988 (sometimes written 8-8-88) may be the luckiest birthdate.

Year of the Dragon: 1976, 1988; healthy, complex, passionate

Year of the Snake: 1977, 1989; wise, high-spirited

Year of the Horse: 1978, 1990; popular, impatient

Year of the Sheep: 1979, 1991; elegant, creative, private

Year of the Monkey; 1980, 1992; intelligent, enthusiastic

Year of the Cock: 1981, 1993; eager to learn, pioneering

Year of the Dog: 1982, 1994; loyal, stubborn, generous

Year of the Boar: 1983, 1995; noble, feisty, a friend for life

Year of the Rat: 1984, 1996; ambitious, funloving, freespending

Year of the Ox: 1985, 1997; bright, patient, inspiring

Year of the Tiger: 1986, 1998; courageous, open, sensitive

Year of the Rabbit: 1987, 1999; lucky, peace seeking, talented

The Chinese also assign animals with special qualities to the hours of the day. The time at which you are born determines which animal's qualities you will inherit.

11 P.M.–1 A.M.	Hours of the Rat
1–3 A.M.	Hours of the Ox
3–5 A.M.	Hours of the Tiger
5–7 A.M.	Hours of the Rabbit
7–9 A.M.	Hours of the Dragon
9–11 A.M.	Hours of the Snake
11 A.M.–1 P.M.	Hours of the Horse
1–3 P.M.	Hours of the Sheep
3–5 P.M.	Hours of the Monkey
5–7 P.M.	Hours of the Cock
7–9 P.M.	Hours of the Dog
9–11 P.M.	Hours of the Boar

CHAPTER

14

Pets

ON FARMS around Changsha, families have pigs, ducks, geese, chicks. They have great muddy water buffaloes that children ride to water holes and bathe and boss and grumble at. The occasional farm family has a dog.

City folk have few animals. Older people remember dogs from their childhoods and speak fondly of them. But food is expensive and apartments are small. And keeping the city clean is an awful task already. City Chinese have had to agree: Dogs are a luxury they cannot have.

Some people keep fish or crickets. A few have cats. Birds are the pets of choice. Many people have them—colorful little parakeets and canaries and big brown thrushes—strong singers, all. In the mornings, early, bird owners are out and about through the city taking birds for airings. They carry the birds in cages and keep the cage covers pulled down along the way to protect their pets against bewilderment on the journey.

In the parks, bird people flock together. They hang their cages from branches where the birds have companions. Then they stand aside, to do *tai chi* exercise. Or they smoke and chat or peacefully breathe out and breathe in while the birds catch healthful breaths also and hop about, singing. Birds sometimes sing solo or in a duet. Often the birds sing all together. Their chorus fills the air. It floats over park walls to early-bird passersby on the sidewalk, who hear it on their way to school or to work.

This retired couple specializes in selling birds called spectacled laughing thrushes. (The spectacles are natural eyepatches. The laugh is part of their fine song.) Husband and wife collect the birds on trips to the country and sell them for eighteen Chinese dollars, maybe three days' pay. They say a thrush song gladdens the heart.

CHAPTER

¤ 15 ¤

One Child

ON AN OUTDOOR bulletin board, with neighborhood news and snap-shots, a cartoon strip looks playful and carries a strong message. In Square One a husband and wife happily paddle their boat, looking pleased with each other, pleased with their progress. Musical notes fly from the husband's mouth. He's whistling or he's singing. By Square Two, time has passed. There's a bright-eyed child on his mother's lap. The mother holds him and plays with him. The father, paddling solo, looks proud and serious. Musical notes have vanished. Square Three, more time has passed. Now the mother has a lapful—three children, clearly more than she can handle on this small craft. Everyone looks cross. The children are squabbling. Father paddles hard, with beads of sweat pouring from his brow.

The message is: For each couple in China there shall be one

Grandfather and grandson spend long hours in each other's company—an arrangement that seems to suit both of them.

COCO'S FAMILY

When the Fan family is at home Sundays, little Coco has only to raise his arms to be lifted; or reach down toward a cup for it to be placed in his hands; or shake his head side to side, no, to the offer of juice and up and down, yes, to the offer of an orange. At fifteen months, he's the first great-grandchild. He's not spoiled, but he's not neglected either.

Coco knows who will hold him up to see pictures or a river rock on the cupboard (*po po* is the Chinese word for a grandmother on the father's side). The baby knows who will sing to him funny and exciting songs and swing him through the air (*shu shu* means uncle on the father's side, *shen shen* is aunt), who will line up sticks for him and count them (*ye ye* means father's father).

Coco's eyes dart to the person as the name is spoken. As for *ma ma* and *ba ba*, Coco says the names himself. He says *wai po* also, for the second grandmother. When he wants to be out on adventures, he tugs at her clothing. Home for her is a dormitory at the factory where she works, so she can't invite him to stay with her. But she too loves the sidewalks, and she comes daily to take him on outings. *Wai po* is mother's mother.

In this household it's the *tai po po* who is quiet and stays put. She reads her Monkey King novel or she paints or strings beans. Coco has figured out that hers is the lap to climb onto when he's too tired to play and too wide-awake for bed. *Tai po po* is the Chinese name for great-grandmother on the father's side. Coco may also think it means peace.

child only. Since 1980, billboards proclaim it and street committees remind neighbors. Couples who have more children are severely criticized and punished with heavy fines and lost privileges.

As it is in the cartoon boat, the problem is too many people. China, with a fifth of the world's people, doesn't have a fifth of the world's farmland for feeding them.

There's reason for the one-child rule. And Chinese people are used to rules and to a tight control over their lives by their leaders. A man here in the city must be at least twenty-two to marry (a woman, twenty) and the housing for them will come only with a job. People don't just look for a room and rent it, or move to a new city to job hunt, either. Men and women in China try hard

Right: Children on their way home from school, their bookbags bulging with homework and a thermos (for boiled water), take a look at treats for sale. Small stores selling drinks, cigarettes, and snacks now stock jars of penny candies and nuts to attract such youngsters. As only children, they may have bits of money in their pockets.

Bottom: Legs crossed in a man-at-ease fashion, one youngster expresses the joy of an outing with Popsicles for "just my dad and me."

for work that they like, but they expect to take up whatever is assigned. They expect to live with the members of the work unit as their large family.

Changsha parents are quick to say it's good for China to have fewer children. The mother of a ten-year-old says, "It may even be good for *us*"—for mother, father, child. Her husband agrees. "There's money for bits of meat or fish or chicken almost every day with our rice."

All the same, living by the one-child rule is hard. Babies are dearly loved. Large families are a tradition, especially in the countryside, where most Chinese live. On farms children are counted on to help. It's an advantage to have more children—especially, it's thought, if they are strapping boys "to carry the grain."

City parents are apt to grumble that exceptions are made to the rule, often in unfair ways. Many farmers are allowed to have a second child, especially if the first child is a girl, who may be fragile. Parents also feel sad that a child of theirs won't experience life with brothers and sisters. In the next generation, the child of their child won't even have uncles, aunts, cousins. And when the child marries, the young couple will have two sets of aging parents. How will that work out?

Children of course say they're lonesome. With both parents at work six days a week, boys and girls wish for a sister or a brother for company. Adults say that many of today's only children are spoiled. They could come to be a generation of "little emperors," demanding ever more treats and attention.

Other adults see that children may already have more attention than they can handle. To be the One and Only makes children feel wanted. It can also make them feel that the least bit of fooling around they do is a crime and any little dumb mistake is a calamity, and that maybe they will never live up to a family's hopes for them.

I'm an only son. In school I feel lonely. My parents are often on a business trip. If I have a brother I can tell stories to him. I'll crack a joke to him. I'll tell him how to play chess. I'll teach him to play ball. I'll study with him and help him. When he's ten, I'll give him a bike of mine. After that we'll ride bikes to school. A brother can make fun. He can make me confident to do well in my studies. I wish I had a brother.

Ren "Thomas" Liu

⚄ 16 ⚄

Calligraphy

IN THE REN family there are two boys (born before 1980 and the start of the one-child rule). On a Sunday, the Ren boys' father coaches them from the sidelines, cheering them on at their calligraphy. "Not too much ink!" These are words of caution, to protect from inky fingers and blotching. "Work bigger, bigger!" Those are words to encourage bold, loose strokes. In this family, writing in ink with a brush is a Sunday-morning pastime. It's a puzzle, a game. When pages turn out well, they're kept to hang on a wall or to unroll for admiring.

For everyday writing, pencil or pen does fine. But calligraphy, with the brush, is special. It's an art form from ages past and has many styles to it, some of them feathery-looking, some dashing.

"Step back from the table, bend a bit!" is the father's advice—to get a good view of the paper and good action from the shoulder. The right way to hold the brush is straight up and down.

Calligraphers must keep their wits about them and work fast, with a brush that's not too dry and not too wet. Younger brother Yan-ming (his name means Bright Cloud), does well. No splats. And all his strokes are in the right order and in the right direction. Never mind that his writing is still blocky-looking, still a bit wooden. He's eleven. His skills are coming.

Three years older, Long-fei now writes with his wrist up off the page. It gives him an advantage. His name means Flying Dragon, and he truly skims his strokes down the page, to make thick-thin lines that have life and a good flow to them.

With brush and ink there's no going back to correct or improve. A mistake means you must start over with a fresh sheet, which is why the Ren family uses cheap newsprint rather than fine paper. It's also why the children try to concentrate and to keep calm. A careless hand blunders. But a too-tight hand spoils the brushwork also, robbing it of life.

Flying Dragon has learned a showy way to make sharp starts. It's to touch down his brush just below where he wants to start a stroke and then to draw the brush upward and swoosh it back again in a clear wet slash. The father lets out a long breath. He's impressed and he says so.

Father and sons take time-outs to stretch and to pass around their papers and talk about them. "Lopsided here, but not bad there, is it?" They go from sit-down to stand-up writing, at a high table. The boys will see more clearly standing, the father says. They'll write stronger, from the shoulder.

This day they practice "heart" words, folding their papers first to give them guidelines for size. Heart is xin ("shin") and the way to write it is a four-stroke character. Combined with the character for "middle," it makes a new character, "loyalty" or "loyal." A loyal person has

"The Four Valuable Things" are the ink stick, the ink slab (where the stick is rubbed about, to get a thick puddle), the paper, and the brush. "Heart" is the four-stroke character on the lower left. "Small" is the one above it.

his heart well centered. ("Middle" is written as a target pierced with an arrow, just as it is in Middle Kingdom, the name for China.)

In a different way, "small" written along with "heart" makes "careful." To be of small heart is to be careful, timid, cautious. The Chinese put "small heart!" (*shao xin*) on signs at railway crossings and beside stoves.

Calligraphers of course know that life is complex. Even when writing with ink, it is necessary to be of small heart ("Not too much ink!") and to throw caution to the winds ("Work bigger") almost at the same instant.

In the boys' workbook, a "heart" word for "peace" baffles them. It's an old-fashioned way to write it. It baffles their father also, and their mother. Parents and boys try "writing" it, the way Chinese do, invisibly, with the right index finger as a brush and the palm of the left hand as paper. Then they check in the dictionary. Here! It needs one more stroke. Perfect! Puzzling out the words is part of the pleasure for calligraphers. "Heart" plus "roof" plus "cup," put together properly, means peace—a word truly to be pleased with.

From experience the boys know there will be no peace for them if they fail to rinse their brushes in cold water and clean up after the inky morning. There will be no peace if they read comic books before doing homework. But today is free-day Sunday, and calligraphers may settle into Captain Black Cat detective comics till lunch.

CHAPTER

ᴿ 17 ᴳ

Play Days

CHANGSHA'S CITY KIDS say a great lump of schoolwork sits on their shoulders always; they've no time to play. Even the fine noontime breaks from school aren't for hanging out with friends (though hanging out is a favorite Chinese pastime). The breaks are for the *xiu-xi* ("she-you-shee"), the nap. ("We *xiu-xi* whether we want to or not," a sixth grader says. "We're expected to rest or to read"— and not laugh-out-loud books either, but the kind with quizzes at the ends of chapters.

Playtimes, children say, are counted out in short snatches before supper and in Saturday nights and parts of Sundays. Through the weeks before exams, the playtimes are shorter yet. Some parents rule out soccer practice. Or they don't allow bicycle riding. To

Youngsters learn early the pleasures of reading comics and snacking, also the art of the relaxed Chinese flatfoot squat.

Along the street, children with fen (pennies) to spend treat themselves to a filmstrip. They turn a dial to see China's Great Wall and the gorges of the Yangtze River. The cords are to discourage viewers from walking off with the equipment.

Except in the heat of summer, jump rope is enormously popular. Here it's Chinese-style with a rubberband "rope" stretched (ankle high) between two players.

save precious time for study, parents may shift a child to an aunt's apartment close to school. They excuse a child from chores. Never mind that mopping might be a happy change from reviewing math.

All the same, the young people do not look put upon. Out on the streets, in playgrounds, in quiet corners of the compounds, they lark along, joshing with friends, even if it's only as companions in grumbling.

Boys by Changsha's Xiang River on a hot afternoon splash in the shallows or dig bait for fishermen, lifting the worms with chopsticks. At a doorway small girls slap cards onto a tabletop the size

"JUMP ROOMS"

Middle schoolers still find hopscotch ("jump rooms") fun. It's a game worth squabbling about, worth playing with style. Players drop-kick a stone into Square, or Room, One, then into Two, Three, Four. At Five they put both feet down. Electricity and water are hazards. Landing on Dog, Rooster, Joy, or Sorrow means starting afresh and barking, crowing, hahaing, or sobbing all the way. To land in the Freedom square is to win. Are boys or girls better at hopscotch? "Boys," says Louis. "Girls," says Jane, who adds, "Louis is smart and a lovely boy, but at hopscotch girls are best—*ab-so-lute-ly.*"

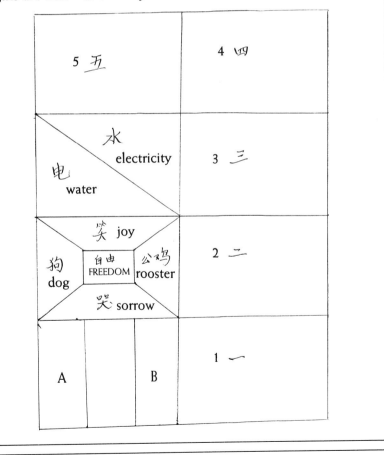

of a hanky. They look competent. (After all, playing cards—and not just fireworks, tea, noodles, Ping-Pong, and paper—are a Chinese invention.) Wherever there are sandpiles at construction sites, youngsters run up and down with pretend weapons, *ack-acking.*

Children play nonstop games of hopscotch and jump rope. They roll hoops with sticks and compete to kick a shuttlecock in the air, counting the kicks. Ping-Pong is played on desk tops and tables of any size, with or without a net. For kites the air is mostly too soggy or too still except in spring.

Chinese chess pieces include a general (in place of the king), officers, statesmen, horse soldiers, chariots, cannons, and foot soldiers. The midline of the board is the river. Four squares at either end of the board represent a palace, which the general may never leave. To capture a general is to win. Children say Western chess is more difficult than Chinese because "If you're careless, you lose at once."

On a school playground, Ping-Pong tables (with cement tops and cement nets) also serve for games of cards. A favorite game, da bai fen, *a kind of rummy, leads to outbursts of joy and grief.*

Movies are a rare treat. The tickets are gotten through parents' work units, in the way that people apply to buy train tickets, oil, rice, or an item in short supply such as a bike.

At home children say they find it hard to lure parents into games with them. They say parents are forever cooking, cleaning, washing; or they're deep in studies of their own.

Family television watching happens more often. Half the city's families have sets. And evening shows include operas, spy stories, war stories, foreign films, lessons (how to dance; how to do percents; how to speak English as the British speak it). Among the

ROLLER-SKATING

Halfway along the bridge across the big brown Xiang River, there's the racket of a jet roar or of thunder. It comes from the rink on Orange Island where crowds of roller skaters hurtle around on a cement floor to loud music. Speed skaters and dancers are the stars. A pair of men in matching red T-shirts glide and twirl with a show of crossed ankles at the turns. Daredevils choose to skate over a roller-coaster portion of the floor, while saner folk steer to either side of it. The novices—and there are many—wobble and lurch, supported by friends. Or they clutch the rail.

Numbers of young soldiers skate here in their green uniforms; numbers of college students, too, from their campuses on the far side of the river. "It costs us only four *jiao* ["jow"] an hour." (*Jiao* are like dimes.) "It's good exercise and fun," one student says. He's gliding off to join his partner, a young woman who moves her feet cautiously, left right left.

big TV hits are Shirley Temple pictures, where the star sings "On the Good Ship Lollipop" in English but speaks Chinese. Another hit is the rerun of a Chinese cartoon starring Shao Ma Hu (Little Horse Tiger), a mixed-up, wildly careless youngster. Young Ma Hu doesn't get the notion to change until in a dream he visits Ma Hu City, where the city wall by mistake has no gate, and cars are missing crucial parts, and everyone is as slapdash as he, including the teacher of math. Weeknights children are mostly shooed away from the television set. Weekends they can negotiate. Over *Donald Duck* time, Sundays, there's no argument.

CHAPTER

⟨ 18 ⟩

Children's Day

EVERY DAY is children's day in China, where children are doted on and treasured, but on June first there's an official Children's Day also. For middle schoolers, it's their chance to collapse and be lazy. Bliss! For elementary-school children it's a day to show off—to march and clap and salute, to sing, and to sit in rows wearing snowy shirts and bright-colored sashes and headbands.

At the Sazi Tang Primary School, children parade before the reviewing stand and take their places on chairs set up two by two on the playing field. Bands play. Honor guards carry the flags. Banners snap in the wind.

This day dawned dark as the bottom of a well. It has lightened up to a Changsha gray, which now is shot through with flickerings of sunlight onto roof tiles and brass instruments.

Elementary-school children celebrating Children's Day honor the marching bands and red flags with a raised right-arm salute (elbow out, palm forward).

A loud loudspeaker amplifies the music and all the prize giving and the speeches. From the stage an old gentleman says he hopes the children are very well. He speaks for the members of his neighborhood old men's association. He hopes the children take care of their bodies so they will live long and in good health. He hopes they will study hard and serve their country always. He is applauded mightily. So is the girl who sings "The Song of the Young Pioneer." (Her name, Yan, means Swallow.) So is a stream of other performers, including the first graders who sing spring songs and fly-to-the-moon songs.

Between numbers there's a lot of cheerful chat in the audience and then some shouts, too, especially with the wind rising and with the sky going dark and light again in turns. The first raindrops promise a cloudburst finish for the celebration.

Through the first drops of rain, youngsters who came prepared reach for jackets, ponchos, umbrellas. Others, when the rain turns serious, hoist chairs overhead for shelter.

Zai Jian, Good-Bye

CHANGSHA DAZZLES after a storm. Even in its everyday gray, Changsha is blessed with its trafficky river and leafy lanes and with bookshops where readers stand elbow to elbow and finish whole books (just browsing, thank you). People who live here say their big city has a small-town feeling. They bicycle from end to end through its hodgepodge of neighborhoods, and they know the sights and the potholes to expect along the way, the laundry, and the games of hopscotch chalked across pavements. Neighbors know each other's business.

From the look of it, life here for children is lean and spare. The belongings of any one of them could fit in a box on the back of a bicycle with room left over for a soccer ball. The happenings in their lives are school and home and trips in between.

From the look of it also, life is interesting. Faces are lively-looking, amused and curious.

If, among themselves, young people shrug and laugh and say "BORING" about school, they mean it and they don't mean it—both. All the drill in class and the practice-makes-perfect attitude can be hard to accept. Their language takes a lifetime to puzzle out. They begin to see: It gives a lifetime's delight.

School kids say "BORING" partly just to use a new favorite word in English. They don't much say it at home. Who would? For the cheerful grown-ups they care about—the parents and great-aunts—have all survived violence and turmoil. They've known awful times in their childhoods, when everyday school, one day like the next, would have been bliss. Who'd want to sound whiny to them?

The good luck of the city's children (they know it) is to live as they have lived with years, all in a row, of peace. There's jump rope in their lives and television and cards, comic books, and splashing in the river. From loudspeakers, music floats across their compounds—Chinese opera, Bach, "Hark the Herald Angels Sing." Not slogans and a harsh summons to meetings, as in years past. Look-alike clothes have vanished. In children's memory, life for families has lightened and brightened. It has gotten more prosperous—here a violin and there a refrigerator.

Not everyone looks happy—not bone-weary people on the street hauling loads. Not crabby clerks at ticket windows. Or teenagers without jobs, either. China's struggle to be a modern country is still a rough one. Yet through the children's school years, life has opened bit by bit—to world news and to foreign nonsense like Donald Duck. People have come to expect the freedom to buy and to sell in open markets, and to move, some, in and out of the city, and to speak their minds about wishes for change and for fairness from their leaders.

College students have taken to Changsha's streets—in goodwill—with banners, demonstrating for more choice in what they will study and become in their lives. They did it in June of 1989, when great masses of students and workers demonstrated in China's capital, and when hundreds were killed there by the Army in one frightful night. That crackdown has shaken the Chinese people and shaken China's friends everywhere. It was the kind of brutality that parents and teachers feared might happen here in Changsha. And Changsha students knew the risk of it.

Schoolchildren watched and listened. They do so now. Risk is not beyond their experience. To race down a paper with a brush of ink takes a kind of risk they know. To stare down an opponent at *wushu,* or to somersault with sabers, demands daring. So does singing before strangers or standing in the hush of a classroom to recite.

Such daring (and the too-much homework) is expected of children daily. Much is hoped for them. Then there's the children's own hope—one day to help China and to find that their help is welcome.

Index

Numbers in *italics* refer to illustrations